Set design by Jeff Robinson

Photo by Mitchell Haddad

Val Lauren, Larry Clark and Bre Blair
in the Mineral Theatre Company production of *Two Wrongs*.

TWO WRONGS

BY SCOTT CAAN

★

DRAMATISTS
PLAY SERVICE
INC.

For Bob and Playhouse West
Thank you for everything

and to Mike O'Malley
Love ya Dools

TWO WRONGS was originally produced at the Mineral Theatre Company (Mike O'Malley, Producer) in Los Angeles, California, on April 23, 2010. It was directed by Missy Yager; the set design was by Jeff Robinson; the lighting design was by Russell Boast; the sound design was by Steve Altman; and the stage manager was Rebecca Schoenberg. The cast was as follows:

SHELLY .... Bre Blair
JULIAN .... Larry Clarke
TERRY .... Val Lauren

CHARACTERS

SHELLY

JULIAN

TERRY

PLACE

A therapist's office.

TIME

The present.

TWO WRONGS

ACT ONE

Scene 1

The waiting room of a therapist's office. Lights up on a man, mid-thirties, sitting alone with his legs crossed.

A woman, thirty, walks in the door. She sees him, immediately turns her head, and faces the other direction.

WOMAN. Oh shit, I'm sorry. *(The man stands up.)*
MAN. It's fine. *(The woman still faces the other direction.)*
WOMAN. What are you doing here?
MAN. I don't know. What are you doing here?
WOMAN. I come here. This is my time. Why are you here?
MAN. I thought this was my time. What time is it?
WOMAN. My time for sure. You got the wrong time. I'm very neurotic about times. This is definitely mine.
MAN. You can turn around and look at me if you want.
WOMAN. I'd rather not. I think we're all clear now. So why don't you just turn for the door and head out, and I'll stay like this 'til you go.
MAN. I really don't mind.
WOMAN. Well, I do. I really mind.
MAN. Okay.
WOMAN. Nothing personal. I'm sure you're great and everything, but I mind for sure. So that's that.
MAN. Okay. *(After a silent beat.)* I'm Terry.
WOMAN. No.

MAN. NO?

WOMAN. Absolutely not.

MAN. Okay.

WOMAN. Nice to meet you.

MAN. We didn't meet.

WOMAN. That's fine too. Have a nice day.

MAN. You sure you don't want to turn around?

WOMAN. Sure. Completely sure. Thank you. *(The man takes a beat, and then heads for the door.)*

MAN. See ya.

WOMAN. Okay. Yes. Have a … nice day.

MAN. Thank you. *(The man walks out of the office, leaving the woman standing alone. Lights out.)*

Scene 2

Therapist's office.

Lights up on an older man sitting in a big recliner. This is Julian.

The man from the last scene sits up on a day bed. Terry.

TERRY. It didn't work. It was terrible.

JULIAN. What happened?

TERRY. She wouldn't even look at me.

JULIAN. Hmm.

TERRY. She seemed crazy.

JULIAN. She's not.

TERRY. She was panicked.

JULIAN. She takes her anonymity very seriously.

TERRY. Is she attractive?

JULIAN. Not because of her physical appearance.

TERRY. I understand that. I'm just asking.

JULIAN. I already told you she was very pretty.

TERRY. And smart. You said that too.

JULIAN. Very smart.

TERRY. But not so together?

JULIAN. I never said that.

TERRY. She almost had a panic attack.

JULIAN. I don't think that's true.

TERRY. You weren't there.

JULIAN. I was listening, and she didn't have a panic attack, nor was she panicking. She just didn't want you to see her.

TERRY. You were listening?

JULIAN. I was.

TERRY. That's weird.

JULIAN. I agree.

TERRY. So now what?

JULIAN. We tried.

TERRY. That's it?

JULIAN. Absolutely.

TERRY. Absolutely not. I want to meet her.

JULIAN. Why?

TERRY. Because she's smart, and pretty.

JULIAN. How do you know that?

TERRY. Because you told me.

JULIAN. I could be wrong.

TERRY. Are you?

JULIAN. I don't think so.

TERRY. Don't do that. Not like this.

JULIAN. I'm sorry.

TERRY. Don't do that either.

JULIAN. Look, it was bad judgment on my part. I apologize. I had an idea, and now I can see, clearly, that it was a bad idea.

TERRY. No no no no. Don't do that.

JULIAN. I just thought …

TERRY. That she was a great girl out there struggling looking for a great guy, and what a great idea. It's still a great idea. Don't do this now. Don't get all professional on me now. This was your idea, you've aroused my curiosity, I'm interested, and now you can't do this.

JULIAN. You have to calm down.

TERRY. I'm perfectly calm. I want to meet her.

JULIAN. Do you understand the position I am in here?

TERRY. Do I understand the position you have put yourself in here? Yes I do.

JULIAN. Really?

TERRY. Absolutely. I didn't come up with this. I didn't say, hey doctor, have any sexy interesting patients to set me up with? Why? Because it's immoral and totally unprofessional. Which is something I thought you would never be. You said it. You brought it up to me.

JULIAN. I understand that, and now I am asking you to see the position I have put myself in, and also take note of the fact that I was trying to help you, while not seeing the very immoral — immoral given the present circumstance — judgment, or rather lack there of, on my part. So I am further asking you to have some compassion, realize human beings are what they are and that they make mistakes. Forgive me. Please let it go.

TERRY. I can't do that, though. Not at this point. I can't do that. I've been sparked. Something in me has been ignited and you of all people should know, if not explored thoroughly, that is a place for me where I will lose sleep.

JULIAN. Furthermore a bad idea in general.

TERRY. But you can't say that.

JULIAN. I just did.

TERRY. But you can't. That's further immoral. It's manipulative. It's using one for the other. You can't do that now.

JULIAN. What do you want me to do?

TERRY. Let's try it again.

JULIAN. I can't do that. I just cannot. She spent half the hour discussing with me the right to her anonymity and how it was broken the other day, and that it was very careless of me, and how could I. It can't happen again.

TERRY. It has to.

JULIAN. It can't. Do you have any idea what it is like to be chastised by one of your patients?

TERRY. No, I don't. I'm not a doctor, I don't have patients.

JULIAN. Well, it's not the way things are supposed to happen.

TERRY. But we crossed the line ... See how I don't blame you? I'm partially responsible, but I can't take all the heat. The heat being my suffering. We're in this together, but we are most certainly in this. I'm not saying it's over when I say so, 'cause that would be immoral on my part, and I don't want to do that. But I'm kind of saying that, because it's just not over yet. I want to see her again. What's her name?

JULIAN. I can't ...

TERRY. Don't.

JULIAN. Shelly.
TERRY. Shelly?
JULIAN. Yes, Shelly.
TERRY. I want to see Shelly again.
JULIAN. You know ...
TERRY. I'm here. I'm sitting right here. We gotta figure something else out. *(Lights out.)*

Scene 3

Therapist's office. Lights up.

Julian sits listening to the woman. Her name is Shelly.

SHELLY. It's inappropriate is all I'm saying. You just don't do that. I mean who does that? *(Shelly waits for a response.)*
JULIAN. This guy.
SHELLY. Who?
JULIAN. Who?
SHELLY. Who apparently wanders aimlessly, through and around the world, without a clue. No standards. Common sense. Tact. No sense of right and wrong. A complete narcissist.
JULIAN. See, I don't know if I agree with you there.
SHELLY. How could you not?
JULIAN. You know narcissism is an incurable clinical condition.
SHELLY. Well, there you go.
JULIAN. No.
SHELLY. No?
JULIAN. No. See, that's my point. You're destroying this guy.
SHELLY. I'm not destroying anyone, I'm telling you what my first impression was.
JULIAN. You called him a narcissist.
SHELLY. Which is an incurable clinical ...
JULIAN. Condition. Right. How do you know that? You see, I personally, wouldn't be able to form that opinion, come to that conclusion, even begin to approach a diagnostic procedure ...

11

SHELLY. Right.

JULIAN. Well, without giving it some real thought, a solid amount of time spent. Certainly not on a first meeting.

SHELLY. I'm a great judge of character.

JULIAN. I'm a doctor.

SHELLY. What are you saying?

JULIAN. Frankly, without giving someone a real chance.

SHELLY. There it is. Now I see what you are getting at and that's not the case here. I'm open to this man. I'm willing to get involved here, but some things are just unacceptable.

JULIAN. He burped.

SHELLY. No he did not. He did not just burp. He blew. Burped and blew. Sideways he blew. It was the motion of his body. It was the way he shifted in his seat as the air left his face. Unacceptable. In a restaurant no less. It was disgusting and I will never look at him the same. First date, third date, that's not the point. It is just what it is.

JULIAN. Is it though? It sounds mysteriously similar to the salad dressing guy who ended up not being so terrible, in my opinion. You continued to destroy him as well, but from what I heard, he seemed okay.

SHELLY. Oh God. The ranch dressing. He was an animal.

JULIAN. He had a little salad dressing in the corners of his mouth.

SHELLY. Did I use the word little? I never said little. And it wasn't just dressing, it was ranch. Ranch is thick, white, and has texture.

JULIAN. I've seen it.

SHELLY. A large portion of thick, white, and textured salad dressing, cascading down from the corner of his gob.

JULIAN. It's all vivid and clear now, thank you.

SHELLY. I'm just saying.

JULIAN. Yes, and I'm just saying.

SHELLY. I get what you are saying.

JULIAN. What am I saying?

SHELLY. People are goofy.

JULIAN. *(Julian shakes his head "NO", and says ...)* Exactly.

SHELLY. And oftentimes repulsive. But maybe, just maybe, tucked away and hidden behind the grotesque and mannerless is a shiny chivalrous gem, so we must give things a chance.

JULIAN. Good. Now, I have to ask you a question.

SHELLY. The burper's out.

JULIAN. That's fine.

SHELLY. Thank you.

JULIAN. Do you remember the guy you saw in the waiting room last week?

SHELLY. You know I do.

JULIAN. Something has come up. Things happen and sometimes they were just written and there's nothing to do but move forward.

SHELLY. What are you talking about?

JULIAN. He's interested.

SHELLY. Interested?

JULIAN. Interested.

SHELLY. In what?

JULIAN. I'm sorry.

SHELLY. What the fuck …

JULIAN. Just listen to me.

SHELLY. I am.

JULIAN. This is nobody's fault.

SHELLY. Everything is somebody's fault. What the hell do you mean, he's interested?

JULIAN. Not everything is someone's fault.

SHELLY. Goddamn it.

JULIAN. Don't be crass.

SHELLY. Damning God is not crass. Certainly not when you don't believe in Him.

JULIAN. I'm trying to say something here.

SHELLY. And …

JULIAN. And if you would let me …

SHELLY. Speak?

JULIAN. Yes, speak. I will explain and you will see the harm has already been done.

SHELLY. What harm? Where is there harm? Who's been harmed?

JULIAN. No one, that is my point.

SHELLY. Harm's way? This man is crazy? What the hell are you saying to me right now?

JULIAN. No harm. That is what I'm saying. The harm has been done, as in there is none. The worst has happened, it's no big deal. Certainly nothing immoral or way out of bounds. A mistake. But this man is interested under the non-fault of no one. The circumstances. The accidental happening last week. He's interested.

SHELLY. What is that? What does that mean?

JULIAN. He's asked about you. *(Shelly takes a beat.)*
SHELLY. He asked about me?
JULIAN. Yes.
SHELLY. In what fashion?
JULIAN. Excuse me?
SHELLY. Why are you being weird?
JULIAN. I'm not being weird. What do you mean weird?
SHELLY. You're being weird.
JULIAN. Am I?
SHELLY. Yes.
JULIAN. Well, maybe because this is something new for me. Something very out of the ordinary, and something I've yet to deal with. But keeping in mind that it's not such a thing, just a happening. Something that is not harmful in any way to any patient. So I'm balancing. I'm balancing my morals with the situation, and as I speak I see the simplicity. I haven't given this a great deal of thought. It's just something that has come up.
SHELLY. Right.
JULIAN. Weird like that, you mean?
SHELLY. I guess.
JULIAN. So?
SHELLY. So?
JULIAN. What do you think?
SHELLY. What do I think about what?
JULIAN. About this guy?
SHELLY. About this guy? I don't think anything about this guy. What could I possibly think about him?
JULIAN. Good. I understand. Let me rephrase. About the situation. What are your feelings on the situation?
SHELLY. The situation? I don't have any. My feelings? I have none. I know nothing, how could I have feelings about something I know nothing about?
JULIAN. Well, see, that's interesting.
SHELLY. What's interesting about it?
JULIAN. Well, I tell you someone's interested.
SHELLY. You find that interesting?
JULIAN. No. I find it interesting that you are not interested.
SHELLY. That I've been found interesting?
JULIAN. Yes.
SHELLY. That's interesting.

JULIAN. Exactly.

SHELLY. This is weird.

JULIAN. You keep saying that.

SHELLY. Because it is. This man who hears my voice. Speaks nothing more than basic pleasantries to the back of my head for less than a minute's time finds me intriguing for some reason. You seem to be supporting this … This circle of sorts. This round robin of dysfunction.

JULIAN. Wait a minute.

SHELLY. The man obviously has issues.

JULIAN. Why is that?

SHELLY. He's here, isn't he?

JULIAN. Everyone should be here. Not here with me specifically, but somewhere.

SHELLY. Desperation. Inappropriate longing. I mean come on.

JULIAN. What's so desperate, and what's inappropriate? You're destroying already.

SHELLY. That's insane. There's nothing to be destroyed.

JULIAN. I'm just saying is all.

SHELLY. What all are you saying?

JULIAN. That this man. This man, that I cannot speak of with any sort of great detail, because of certain moral codes I stand by, has pegged you a target.

SHELLY. A target?

JULIAN. Not in the sense of on which to be fired upon. A source of interest. For whatever reason you've been beckoned, and what's important is not why or what his motives are, and again I could tell you about what an interesting, intelligent and further non-psychotic man he is, but I cannot under the circumstances. You must appreciate that. The point is this. What is worth a look, is the fact that you, rather than seeing the simplicity, and frankly, the harmless potential, the possible romantic side of all this. I mean for all you know this man could be the messiah. But what do you see? Dysfunction. Inappropriate behavior. Destruction! Why is that?

SHELLY. Are you implying that I should go out with this man?

JULIAN. Would that be so terrible? *(Shelly has no response.)* Seriously. I'm asking you. *(Lights out.)*

Scene 4

Exterior of a restaurant.

Lights up on Terry and Shelly sitting on a bench, holding coffees.

TERRY. So.
SHELLY. So?
TERRY. I don't know.
SHELLY. You don't know?
TERRY. This is ...
SHELLY. Strange?
TERRY. Little bit.
SHELLY. Well, here we are.
TERRY. I like you.
SHELLY. You what?
TERRY. I mean, so far. *(Shelly stares at him, and then away.)* I mean not so far because this is really it, so far, but thus far.
SHELLY. Thus far?
TERRY. I think you're beautiful. That's all I am saying. I like that, is what I'm saying.
SHELLY. Thank you.
TERRY. No. Thank you.
SHELLY. For?
TERRY. Being beautiful. And accepting this.
SHELLY. This?
TERRY. This rather strange meeting.
SHELLY. Under the circumstances ...
TERRY. Strange under the circumstances.
SHELLY. Right.
TERRY. I mean if you think about it, it's really not so out there. I mean as these things are to begin with ...
SHELLY. Slightly out there.
TERRY. Sure. But here, because of the way ...
SHELLY. The way?

TERRY. You know what I'm saying.

SHELLY. I do?

TERRY. You don't?

SHELLY. I think I do.

TERRY. Well, sure you do. How could you not?

SHELLY. I don't know.

TERRY. You're testing me.

SHELLY. Look, we don't have to do this.

TERRY. I want to do this, what are you talking about. We're here. I wanted to be here. I'm glad you are here. Let's proceed. Please. I don't care if you are testing me, I mean I care, but it's fine if you are is what I'm saying. I just wanted to know.

SHELLY. Well, what do you mean testing you? Testing you how? What does that mean?

TERRY. I don't know. Like checking or something.

SHELLY. Checking for what, though?

TERRY. For whatever. I don't know.

SHELLY. Well, maybe I am.

TERRY. I'm saying that's fine.

SHELLY. Okay.

TERRY. That's perfectly normal. I suppose I'm doing the same thing.

SHELLY. What, testing me?

TERRY. I suppose.

SHELLY. Well, I don't want to be tested. That's what you're doing? I'm being tested. Graded? What do you mean?

TERRY. I mean we're just doing the same thing. That's all I'm saying.

SHELLY. I guess.

TERRY. So.

SHELLY. So?

TERRY. What do you like to do?

SHELLY. Is there a wrong answer?

TERRY. I'm sure there can be.

SHELLY. What do you like to do?

TERRY. I like your dress.

SHELLY. You seem okay.

TERRY. I think I am.

SHELLY. So am I.

TERRY. Perfect.

SHELLY. Maybe.

TERRY. Maybe.

SHELLY. Maybe not.

TERRY. Maybe not.

SHELLY. You seem relaxed.

TERRY. I am.

SHELLY. So am I.

TERRY. That's good.

SHELLY. I guess so.

TERRY. I think so.

SHELLY. Then tell me something.

TERRY. Okay.

SHELLY. What's wrong with you?

TERRY. Excuse me?

SHELLY. Well, let's get right to it. I mean, people say keep it light, right?

TERRY. Who says?

SHELLY. That's my point. Let's get to it. We're looking here. We're testing. We're relaxed. Why waste time? Why spend the evening discussing records and restaurants? Hobbies and habits. I mean as important as all of that will be, why not get to the core. Work backwards. I mean everyone has something wrong with them. Surely we know what it is. And if we don't, then maybe we should. Am I making sense?

TERRY. I think so.

SHELLY. Then tell me.

TERRY. About what's wrong or about what you are saying?

SHELLY. If you don't know what I'm saying, then we have nothing to talk about.

TERRY. Okay.

SHELLY. I'm not being curt. I'd just like to try honesty. I'm complicated, and I think too much. If that's a bad thing. But like I said I'm relaxed. That's a compliment. To you. I'm complimenting you. I rarely do that, and I rarely find myself in this position. So we could go on about nothing and I can go home wondering, or we can really have a meeting of some substance.

TERRY. Seems very professional.

SHELLY. It's not. It's honest.

TERRY. I get it.

SHELLY. Good, so what's wrong with you?

TERRY. Big test.

SHELLY. Sure. Anyone can handle the little things.

TERRY. I get it.

SHELLY. You're on, and go.

TERRY. I'm not so sure that …

SHELLY. That's a terrible beginning.

TERRY. That this is the best idea in the world.

SHELLY. Sorry.

TERRY. But I am going to give it a shot.

SHELLY. That's good.

TERRY. I can't stand to be alone.

SHELLY. Oh?

TERRY. I mean, I suppose I can stand it, I just don't prefer it.

SHELLY. Why?

TERRY. Something deep.

SHELLY. I imagine so.

TERRY. Sure. And that's the thing. I'm aware of the depth. I feel like I have a pretty solid handle on the background of the situation, but I still am the way that I am. I mean who knows, maybe that never changes.

SHELLY. Maybe.

TERRY. Maybe you go on acting the way that you act but with a greater understanding of things. Seems silly to me, but maybe that's just it. Maybe there is the change. Just knowledge. I mean who really changes anyway?

SHELLY. I'm not really sure either.

TERRY. What about you?

SHELLY. I'd prefer to be alone.

TERRY. On a level …

SHELLY. Deep.

TERRY. Why else?

SHELLY. Sure. But who knows, maybe you're right. Good news for you is you might get lucky one day. Me, I'll just keep wandering around saying no.

TERRY. Maybe I'm wrong.

SHELLY. I hope so.

TERRY. See that. You're already moving forward. *(Shelly takes it in.)*

SHELLY. So should we get something to eat?

TERRY. I don't know, should we? *(She takes a beat to answer.)*

SHELLY. Yes. *(Lights out.)*

End of Act One

ACT TWO

Scene 1

Therapist's office — one month later. Lights up.

Shelly lays in the day bed. Julian sits across from her in the swivel chair.

SHELLY. Oh my God.
JULIAN. There is no God, remember?
SHELLY. There must be.
JULIAN. Really?
SHELLY. I mean …
JULIAN. Where have you been?
SHELLY. I'm really sorry, but …
JULIAN. Don't worry about it.
SHELLY. I just want to say.
JULIAN. You seem …
SHELLY. In a spirit?
JULIAN. Of sorts.
SHELLY. Amazing.
JULIAN. Tell me everything.
SHELLY. This man.
JULIAN. This man?
SHELLY. This man.
JULIAN. Terry?
SHELLY. This Terry. Oh, this man. This Terry.
JULIAN. So that's where you've been. I should have concluded with the dual absence.
SHELLY. I've been filled. Time consumed and worries to the wind, oh my God this man.
JULIAN. You've become poetic.
SHELLY. That's what it is. A poem. Hopefully the longest poem ever put to paper. A modern poem, no paper, and certainly without

20

a pen. One where the author uses a computer. He types away, and when he makes a mistake, he presses rewind, delete, and then starts over with a fresh idea. An idea containing flawless touch and grace. SHUT THE FUCK UP! Who are you? Do you hear me right now?

JULIAN. I do.

SHELLY. I have to thank you, and although you say what you say, I say I'm sorry for not checking in, but I've been, like I said, filled.

JULIAN. It's fine, I just want to hear.

SHELLY. I don't know what to say.

JULIAN. I don't either.

SHELLY. Peace.

JULIAN. Is that a modern goodbye?

SHELLY. No. I feel. That's how I feel. At peace. With everything that's kept me so negative and twisted up for as long as I can remember. But not because of, as a result of, maybe, but not because of. I say that to keep in mind, for you to keep in mind, that it does not feel like, and I could be wrong, but I really don't think so. Like something has opened my eyes. Wide and bright to see what there really is, and what can be. Now, I don't want it to seem as though my problems and my issues have just jumped out of space and flown to nonexistence. They are there, just slightly out of touch. Like a memory that burns, but less and less as the time goes by. One day you feel a burning sensation but you almost can't put a tag on it. You almost don't know if it's really burning. I know I'm rambling on, but I say that, and this, to let you know that I feel getting back in here regularly, is ultimately crucial, and I want you to know that I don't feel fixed, just mended, stitched up, and hopefully on the right track. But I'm here.

JULIAN. That's good.

SHELLY. But ...

JULIAN. Slow down.

SHELLY. I'm speeding aren't I?

JULIAN. Slightly.

SHELLY. That's what it feels like, though.

JULIAN. That's when you need to slow.

SHELLY. Down.

JULIAN. Right. Take a breath. *(Shelly takes a deep breath.)*

SHELLY. Funny how that works. The actual process. The conscious act of doing. Singularly, I mean. Refreshing really.

JULIAN. Good. *(She takes another deep breath.)*

SHELLY. Okay. Now. I also would like to say that in no way is this man perfect.

JULIAN. Sure.

SHELLY. But I accept. I see flaws and they are discussed and the simplicity. You said that.

JULIAN. I did.

SHELLY. The simplicity of I just like you, and I don't care if you burp. I mean I'd rather you not, but we can talk about it, we conclude. You know what I mean?

JULIAN. I do.

SHELLY. It's a constant conclusion with this man. Everything has an ending, or rather a head. A point at which we rest. A resting point at which all the angst and all the pushing for the other direction can cease. For me. Finally. Peace. Now I'm repeating myself.

JULIAN. And once again approaching the speed limit.

SHELLY. Well, then give me a ticket, 'cause I just feel what I feel … Like a fucking woman! Excuse me.

JULIAN. It's fine.

SHELLY. It's crass, I know, as is the damning of God if you believe in that sort of thing, which for all I know, maybe I do. But so you know, I'm holding back.

JULIAN. Well, don't do that.

SHELLY. I must.

JULIAN. That's okay too.

SHELLY. He takes me places I want to go, he holds me the way I want to be held, and God bless him he fucks me like I want to be fucked.

JULIAN. Okay.

SHELLY. I'm sorry.

JULIAN. You must.

SHELLY. I must?

JULIAN. Hold back. You said you must.

SHELLY. I am.

JULIAN. Oh.

SHELLY. Are you uncomfortable?

JULIAN. Not slightly.

SHELLY. Yes you are.

JULIAN. Fine.

SHELLY. I'll hold back.

JULIAN. Now? You'll hold back now?

SHELLY. I was.

JULIAN. Right.

SHELLY. Slightly.

JULIAN. Okay.

SHELLY. Should we continue?

JULIAN. Please.

SHELLY. Okay. I mean I've been there, you know. I've had the experiences, but not like this. And I know that this must be something I've wanted because I've never wanted it, you know? I mean, to be made to feel this way.

JULIAN. You have or have not?

SHELLY. Both. I mean I never wanted it, but now I do. Every day. A lot. As much as possible.

JULIAN. Oh, okay.

SHELLY. Is this too much?

JULIAN. No. It's just the right amount. I mean, it's fine.

SHELLY. Do you have that?

JULIAN. Do I have...?

SHELLY. That kind of sex in your life?

JULIAN. That's not really ...

SHELLY. You know, a partner that pulls and pushes that in and out of you.

JULIAN. Not, not, not really.

SHELLY. Well you should.

JULIAN. We shouldn't ...

SHELLY. Talk about you?

JULIAN. Right.

SHELLY. But it's casual.

JULIAN. Excuse me?

SHELLY. I mean it's okay. Not casual like it's a casual conversation. Nor the sex for that matter. But one that's ... What's the word?

JULIAN. Inappropriate?

SHELLY. No no no. To discuss this with someone would be ...

JULIAN. Inappropriate.

SHELLY. No. With you, maybe, but speaking with someone normal, or abnormal in this case, it would call for some reciprocity. That's the word. Like some sort of bouncing back and forth.

JULIAN. But ...

SHELLY. Not here, I know, but it's just something that happens. So I apologize.

JULIAN. It's fine.

SHELLY. So, just generally, you know what I'm talking about?

JULIAN. The act of … *(Motions with his hands.)*

SHELLY. Yes.

JULIAN. Why don't we just …

SHELLY. Continue?

JULIAN. Please.

SHELLY. Where was I?

JULIAN. I'm not sure.

SHELLY. Are you sure you're okay with this? You seem uncomfortable. I'm totally comfortable, even if you just have to listen with nothing to offer.

JULIAN. Well, I would hope that I have something to offer.

SHELLY. I don't mean like that.

JULIAN. I know you don't mean like that.

SHELLY. Not like that. I mean like in the sense of some feedback.

JULIAN. That's exactly what I was talking about.

SHELLY. Can I just be very honest?

JULIAN. Yes. You can be very honest.

SHELLY. I have been opened up in many ways.

JULIAN. Well, that's good.

SHELLY. Sexually.

JULIAN. Good. That's great. I'm getting that.

SHELLY. Other ways too, but this is what I'm talking about right now. Right here. I mean it's all connected. We connect. Attunement. Both parts. You've spoke of this. Human being to human being on one level, animal to animal on the other. But they bleed. And mesh. It's like one for the other. Don't you think?

JULIAN. I think that, yes.

SHELLY. I feel that I have arrived and landed.

JULIAN. That's hot.

SHELLY. What?

JULIAN. What? *(Shelly takes a beat.)*

SHELLY. Am I safe here?

JULIAN. Safe?

SHELLY. I mean I don't think someone is going to kill me, but I've been feeling slightly neurotic lately, about all of this. Speedy, really. And I want to be able to speak to you, 'cause If I can't speak to you, who is there to speak to?

JULIAN. I'm listening.

SHELLY. That's good, because I'm talking.

JULIAN. Well, that's perfect then.

SHELLY. Are you getting frustrated with me?

JULIAN. Not at all.

SHELLY. 'Cause I need to be supported here. This is all very new for me, and exciting and all these other things, but I need to feel safe.

JULIAN. You're safe.

SHELLY. Because as I'm feeling these feelings, these new feelings, I'm simultaneously having the feeling of feelings, I don't want to feel.

JULIAN. Lot of feelings.

SHELLY. Regret. Like I've been doing it all wrong from the beginning, and what a waste of however many years ... Forget that, right?

JULIAN. Totally.

SHELLY. Why go there?

JULIAN. 'Cause now it feels right.

SHELLY. Everything. There's this balance. This overwhelming sense of balance, not that it's obvious from where you are sitting, but it's incredible. Not to mention I'm having orgasms in my sleep. I feel like Superwoman. Like the greatest thing of all time. Like some creation of superior being.

JULIAN. You look really amazing.

SHELLY. What?

JULIAN. I was going to tell you that, but it felt a little inappropriate, and now you've said it. Or something like it, so I thought I'd chime in. But you really do look amazing. I was going to say that before, but I've already said that. Never mind. Go on.

SHELLY. Thank you.

JULIAN. You're welcome.

SHELLY. I was saying?

JULIAN. Sex. Orgasm. Sleeping. You were sleeping.

SHELLY. Are you okay?

JULIAN. Absolutely.

SHELLY. It's noticeable. I mean that's what you were saying, right?

JULIAN. What is?

SHELLY. Me. This state.

JULIAN. Absolutely. That's what I was saying.

SHELLY. Right. I just feel different.

JULIAN. Difference. Change is the end, or the beginning, or both, of something.

SHELLY. That's it. Change. The end of one and the start of a new.

I am forever changed. A beaming and wonderfully new woman. A catch. Finally! Something I would want for myself. I like me.
JULIAN. I like you too.
SHELLY. And not to go on, but I insist on getting it out, because God knows, if He exists, it's been coming in. My body is glowing and there are no rules. Hit me, touch me, slap me, ravish me, make me wear a costume, do what you will, I accept, because I am your lover. I am your lover to be thrown about or caressed, and fuck it, I might even start cooking. *(Julian is speechless.)* What do you think? *(Lights out.)*

Scene 2

Therapist's office. Lights up.

Terry sits up in the day bed. Julian leans back in his chair.

TERRY. This is impossible.
JULIAN. I'm sorry.
TERRY. But it's impossible. Your being sorry does nothing for something so inconceivable. It's like a bad movie. Bad fiction where the characters jump from building to building missing absolute death. They would die, so why the hell is this happening?
JULIAN. Things happen sometimes, and certain people have certain things.
TERRY. I don't know what that means. What people? Movie people? What are you talking about?
JULIAN. Real people in real life.
TERRY. No. They don't do this, and they don't have these things. What things? What are these things we're talking about?
JULIAN. Issues, Terry.
TERRY. What did she say?
JULIAN. I told you what she said.
TERRY. I know that. And then I told you, not yesterday we held hands and walked through a park. You think that's something I do regularly? Walk through parks holding people's hands?
JULIAN. Actually, I do.

TERRY. Well, I have. But that's not the point. This is different. I've held hands, I've made promises, but not like this.

JULIAN. Why is this different?

TERRY. I don't know why, but it just is. It felt calm. It felt as if it didn't have to be. It wasn't satiating it was real. It felt ... Wait a minute. Why is it felt? It's not felt, it's feel. Not ten minutes ago it was feel, and now it's felt. This is bullshit. What did she say?

JULIAN. I told you ...

TERRY. What she said, I know. And now I'm telling you she must have been kidnapped by the people that make bad movies, because this is not happening. I need specifics. Did she sound drugged? I mean what the fuck?

JULIAN. You know I'm going to have to be honest.

TERRY. That's good.

JULIAN. You seem to me, to be running on in a way.

TERRY. In a way?

JULIAN. A way that we've seen before.

TERRY. What way?

JULIAN. This way. This anxious need for something, someone, that frankly isn't really what they are, but rather what you make them out to be.

TERRY. Not here. Not like that. Not now. Don't.

JULIAN. But why not?

TERRY. I'll tell you why not.

JULIAN. Good, because to me, this seems to be no different than anything else we've seen. I mean, here's this woman who you meet in a waiting room, not even face to face.

TERRY. You can't do that. You cannot do that!

JULIAN. Okay, let me rephrase. As your analyst, the situation, the facts that are what they are ...

TERRY. As sometimes things just are.

JULIAN. Yes, and I suppose I can accept that.

TERRY. Accept it? You played the part. You were the leading man here, Julian.

JULIAN. Doctor Nourmand.

TERRY. No, it's Julian. Today it's Julian. You are no longer this grand God. You no longer sit above dictating and listening. You exist. You maneuver and you play.

JULIAN. That's not fair.

TERRY. Neither is this situation.

JULIAN. Wait a minute.

TERRY. For what? I got nowhere to go. Nothing to do but reach the bottom. Here we are. Here it is.

JULIAN. Fine, but I refuse to sit and play the blame game with you. I refuse to go backwards. What's done is done, and today my part will have been played. I got myself in this position, I admit, and regret, but now I am here, and my final words, and final match- making play for the rest of my psychological career, is, or are. She doesn't want to see you again, nor call, nor write. That was that. I'm sorry, and life can be. That's that. It just can be. Now, to move forward, as Doctor Nourmand, not Julian, I say let it go. Why? Because the real issue here remains to be health. Your health. You spent less than a month with this woman. She wants it to end, she wants it to end. You should be able to accept that, accept it and move on.

TERRY. Fine, but ...

JULIAN. Wait. The fact that you can't, the fact that the attachment is so deep, can only lead me to believe that you are where you were, and this is no different. Another fix, another woman, another grasp for something that you apparently are not yet ready to have.

TERRY. Okay.

JULIAN. Okay?

TERRY. Okay. I think that's bullshit on so many levels, but I say okay.

JULIAN. That's a start.

TERRY. I say it, because there is more. I also argue, maybe at a later date when the bottom of this has been scrapped, bullshit. I spoke of ease, I spoke of something different, and I only wish I would have been here steadily for the last month so that maybe you could have seen it. You see this. This old way. The way of the rug having been pulled. How else should I be? Of course it's a repeat? This is my life. This right here. Not that.

JULIAN. So why the time off, then?

TERRY. What?

JULIAN. Why not stay here?

TERRY. Because I was wrapped up. I was involved and enjoying. I assume you've had the feeling.

JULIAN. That's not ... I don't know.

TERRY. Well, maybe not. Maybe you haven't. And maybe that's why you don't see.

JULIAN. This is not about me.

TERRY. I agree.

JULIAN. So then what are we talking about?

TERRY. We are talking about the time off that I took, we both took, her and I, to enjoy each other and stop thinking. The enrollment in therapy is a full-time job.

JULIAN. As it should be.

TERRY. So we took a break. My idea ... To return, her idea. For this? Is that what you're telling me?

JULIAN. Maybe.

TERRY. Impossible.

JULIAN. She said what she said.

TERRY. But why to you? Why to you, to tell me? I mean as her therapist don't you tell her that this is not the way? For her own well-being and health. I mean come on. Don't you tell her that she's to discuss this with me?

JULIAN. Under normal circumstances, yes I do.

TERRY. Well, why not now?

JULIAN. Because of the situation.

TERRY. Forget the situation. For health purposes. Who does this? Don't you tell her that she has to discuss this with the other human she's actually involved with? I mean, what the hell is wrong with her?

JULIAN. Well, off the record, plenty. But that is not your concern.

TERRY. Sure it is. How is it not?

JULIAN. Because I am playing two parts here. The messenger, to which I have resigned, and her doctor, which is not a file for you to read.

TERRY. But she has to be crazy.

JULIAN. So then what's the problem?

TERRY. It's insane.

JULIAN. Again.

TERRY. What an asshole. How could she do this?

JULIAN. People have their things.

TERRY. I hate her things. I hate that she would do this. How could she do this? What a case.

JULIAN. Now you are making sense.

TERRY. I'm calming.

JULIAN. I see that.

TERRY. Fine. So now that we're settling in a bit, I want to know what she said. *(Julian doesn't respond.)* I don't care what she said. What do I do?

JULIAN. This is good.

TERRY. She said she doesn't want to speak to me anymore. Just like that. Zero. Finished. Nice to meet you? Incorrect! Wrong. Things were on a path. This was a start. Something fresh and futuristic. Not like that but you know what I mean. To be looked forward to, something else. Something with a pulse. She's lost her mind.

JULIAN. Let's move on.

TERRY. To what? Move on to what?

JULIAN. You've gained.

TERRY. Gained what?

JULIAN. Experience.

TERRY. Trauma.

JULIAN. Life is this.

TERRY. This sucks.

JULIAN. Does it really?

TERRY. Sure. Why doesn't it?

JULIAN. Because you learn. You move forward. It's a circle of highs and lows and you find the middle one day.

TERRY. Okay. I'm gonna ask the same question again.

JULIAN. Who knows from good and bad? Lucky, unlucky. All we can do is be, and look ahead. Act civil of course. Grow through any number of chosen ... houses. Houses that house ... growth. You've chosen this one. My house. Therapy. I say you're doing great. Let's move on.

TERRY. I swear to God, I'm gonna fire you in two seconds.

JULIAN. Alright, I need you to listen to me. A man lives alone with his son. They own a small ranch just outside of ... Somewhere. This is not modern.

TERRY. What are you talking about?

JULIAN. I'm making a point.

TERRY. I'm making an exit. Exiting and calling Shelly. I just can't grasp this. Or accept it. Or something. It's too real. Or too fake ... Or something. I don't know. I have to call her.

JULIAN. She doesn't want that.

TERRY. And I don't want this.

JULIAN. You have to listen to me.

TERRY. Do you prescribe?

JULIAN. You know I don't.

TERRY. I think I'm gonna need.

JULIAN. Take a breath.

TERRY. Oh, I hate that.

JULIAN. Breathing?

TERRY. Like without an intention, yes. The act of just doing, yes. Just doing it to concentrate or just for entertainment is shitty.

JULIAN. You have to breathe.

TERRY. I know that. Everybody knows that. That's my point. Why can't we just do it. Multitask. It's an easy one. Why this need to focus or isolate. Just do it and continue on with whatever it was you were doing before.

JULIAN. Fine. Will you listen to me?

TERRY. Yes. And I will continue to breathe simultaneously.

JULIAN. A man lives on a ranch with his son, they own a horse.

TERRY. What kind of horse?

JULIAN. It doesn't matter.

TERRY. It matters. To me it matters. At this point it does.

JULIAN. A quarterhorse.

TERRY. Nice. Like a rodeo horse?

JULIAN. Not like a rodeo horse. Are you being difficult?

TERRY. Not in the slightest. I'm a visionary. I don't want to be filling in the blanks here. My imagination is way too scattered right now, I can only imagine you're making a point, so I'd hate for you to give me the wrong idea.

JULIAN. We are pre-rodeo times here.

TERRY. That's a long time ago. Rodeo dates back to the late 1800s. Imagine that?

JULIAN. Yes, and if you could imagine this. I will leave out details when I feel they are not applicable to the making of my point.

TERRY. I can accept that.

JULIAN. One day the horse runs away.

TERRY. That's fucked.

JULIAN. That's what the neighbor says. What bad luck he says, the farmer simply replies, who knows. Could be bad luck, could be good luck.

TERRY. I hate optimism. Or optimistic people. They lack in modern reality. It's phony.

JULIAN. That's not what this is about. Three days later the horse returns with two wild horses trailing behind.

TERRY. What a nice story. Who doesn't love a happy ending. Be optimistic and you too can invent the rodeo.

JULIAN. It's not over. The neighbor says what good luck, the farmer replies, who knows, could be good luck, could be bad luck. Two days after that, the farmer's son is thrown from one of the new horses while trying to break the wild beast, and shatters his arm at impact.

TERRY. Could be good luck, could be bad luck.

JULIAN. And two days after that, the army shows up to take all the young boys off to war, but the boy with the broken arm could not go.

TERRY. And then all the soldiers get medals of honor, become rich, and buy out all the poor farmers and broken armed children in the neighborhood, leaving them homeless, hungry, and fucked basically.

JULIAN. I don't usually take it that far, but it's possible, yes.

TERRY. Hopefully somewhere down the line someone finds a girlfriend or maybe even a wife. I get your point and it's not a bad one. I'm just having a hard time with the order in which all this has happened. It's goofy, I dare you to argue this.

JULIAN. I won't but what I'm saying is maybe, just maybe it's for the best. You don't know. I think so, but that's me knowing too much, that shouldn't even be a factor, and under normal circumstances would not be. I say take advantage of that, but please for the sake of my job and livelihood, keep it to yourself.

TERRY. She's crazy?

JULIAN. I'm not saying that but, yes.

TERRY. I dodged a bullet here?

JULIAN. Same answer.

TERRY. Leave it alone, and don't call?

JULIAN. Absolutely not. Not call. You are correct.

TERRY. Okay, what about me?

JULIAN. In what sense?

TERRY. I feel like I've failed. If not because of the obvious, the fact that it's a failure in the sense of back to the drawing board. A failure as if, you've gone nowhere, and yet again you have nothing to show for it but general bad taste and a broken picker.

JULIAN. I wouldn't worry about that.

TERRY. Why not?

JULIAN. Because every time you do something incorrectly, you're one step closer to not doing it again.

TERRY. It really seemed right.

JULIAN. I'm sure.

TERRY. What do I do?

JULIAN. Move on and grow. We'll work here, and we'll find the compass, that I can promise. Maybe being alone, I mean really being alone for a little while could be the best thing. *(Terry stands up.)* You're not going to call her, are you?

TERRY. No.

JULIAN. Keep in mind that I feel it would be detrimental if you did.

TERRY. On what level?

JULIAN. All.

TERRY. This all feels very unethical, you know.

JULIAN. I know.

TERRY. Okay.

JULIAN. There's plenty of fish …

TERRY. Don't. Don't do that one. *(Julian stands up.)* I'll see you next week. *(Lights out.)*

End of Act Two

ACT THREE

Scene 1

Therapist's office — one year later. Lights up.

Julian sits behind his desk reading a book.

A knock at the door. Unusual.

He gets up and heads for the door. He opens it. Shelly walks in carrying a large paper bag.

JULIAN. Hey.

SHELLY. Sorry.

JULIAN. No, I'm happy to see you, it's just unusual to have a knock at that door.

SHELLY. I knew it was lunch time so I thought I'd surprise you with lunch. *(He kisses her.)*

JULIAN. I love a surprise lunch.

SHELLY. Good.

JULIAN. What about a surprise sex act before the surprise lunch? *(They stay close.)*

SHELLY. Do you have a patient?

JULIAN. I do.

SHELLY. When?

JULIAN. Too soon.

SHELLY. I couldn't do it in here anyway. It would be too weird.

JULIAN. For you or me?

SHELLY. Hopefully for both of us. It's weird being here at all. I haven't been in here …

JULIAN. Since the last time you were in here, nine months ago, when I asked you out. Which, just to reiterate, I hope you don't share, or have not yet shared, with your new therapist.

SHELLY. Why not?

JULIAN. For a number of reasons, the least important being that we've had this conversation eighteen times, and the most important being that it's illegal.

SHELLY. And immoral.

JULIAN. That I don't agree with. You're a stunningly beautiful, intellectual woman and I'm only human.

SHELLY. He would disagree.

JULIAN. That I'm human? No. *(Julian gives her a look.)*

SHELLY. I didn't tell him. I'm taking the liberty to speak for him as he is in the dark, nor is he present. But I assure you he would not approve, being slightly more conservative than you.

JULIAN. What do you think?

SHELLY. I've brought you lunch, Julian, and would most likely sleep with you in one of the most psychologically unhealthy environments in the history of the therapeutic practice. *(Julian grabs her.)*

JULIAN. I'm aroused by the placement and use of your words.

SHELLY. Well, calm yourself, because I said most likely, and it would be just too weird.

JULIAN. I'm open.

SHELLY. You're working.

JULIAN. Hard.

SHELLY. Patient. *(Julian smiles. Thinks then stops smiling.)*

JULIAN. Shit patient.

SHELLY. You okay?

JULIAN. Slightly.

SHELLY. What's the matter?

JULIAN. What do you mean?

SHELLY. What?

JULIAN. I'm fine. *(Julian pushes her away and starts to pace.)*

SHELLY. Okay.

JULIAN. Okay, I have a patient. You have to go.

SHELLY. Okay. That's fine.

JULIAN. You better hurry, 'cause he's a weird one. *(Julian pushes her toward the door. All of a sudden the sound of a door opening and closing is heard offstage.)* Shit, he's early. *(Julian pulls her away from the door.)* What now? There's no way out.

SHELLY. Would you relax.

JULIAN. I'm completely relaxed. You relax.

SHELLY. Right, sorry. *(Julian bites his hand.)* Are you okay?

JULIAN. I'm fine. There's an explanation.

SHELLY. To what?

JULIAN. Solution. No need to explain, just solution. Find one, I mean.

SHELLY. Your patient.

JULIAN. Is in the waiting room.

SHELLY. So ...

JULIAN. So we have to think.

SHELLY. How 'bout the truth?

JULIAN. The truth? What do you mean, the truth?

SHELLY. Your girlfriend brought you lunch. Just tell him on the way out. Explanation. The truth.

JULIAN. The truth can be frightening sometimes.

SHELLY. I hate to keep asking you if you're okay, but are you, because you seem not.

JULIAN. Okay? I'm fine. This is just something. That's what it is. Something that you of all people should not take lightly.

SHELLY. Why is that? You are being ridiculous right now.

JULIAN. Am I? I mean, am I really? Who's the liberal now, huh?

SHELLY. What?

JULIAN. This is serious, and you know it.

SHELLY. Have you been seeing your therapist?

JULIAN. Don't patronize me.

SHELLY. Well, we have to do something here, and it ends with me going that way, so man up.

JULIAN. Don't do that either.

SHELLY. Well. I mean. Come on. It's not that big of a deal.

JULIAN. How can you say that? Not to mention the rules. The ethics behind the institution, the promise made. The pact installed between patient and doctor. The line in the sand where, here, you do not cross. You of all people should respect and appreciate that.

SHELLY. Well, as a matter of fact, I do, and did, and if you recall, personally experienced the crossing of that very line.

JULIAN. That's exactly my point. That's exactly my point. *(Something dawns on Shelly.)*

SHELLY. Who's out there?

JULIAN. An entire world of human beings just trying to figure it all out.

SHELLY. Who's the patient?

JULIAN. That's classified.

SHELLY. It's Terry, isn't it. *(Julian casually walks behind his desk and pretends to look at a piece of paper.)*
JULIAN. It is, by God. How did you know that? *(Shelly calms and then smiles.)*
SHELLY. You're sweet.
JULIAN. What?
SHELLY. You're protecting me. *(Shelly walks over and hugs him.)*
JULIAN. I am? I am.
SHELLY. You don't have to protect me from him.
JULIAN. I don't?
SHELLY. No. I'm so far past that. You of all people should know. You're basically the one who pulled me through. I could look at that man, smile, say hello, and not feel a thing. Certainly no animosity. That was a long time ago, and I grew so much because of it. I'd actually like to thank him for what he did.
JULIAN. I don't think that's necessary. There's another way out of this I'm sure.
SHELLY. I'm fine. I promise.
JULIAN. I just feel that on so many different levels that this is a bad idea for all involved.
SHELLY. Well, I disagree one hundred percent. I think that it would be the first normal action that has taken place here.
JULIAN. In a perfect world, which this is not, maybe.
SHELLY. One-on-one communication, with zero emotion. It's due.
JULIAN. You have no idea.
SHELLY. I have every idea. Finally falling for someone after thinking it wasn't possible and then being told it's over, not even to my face, having his therapist, you, tell me ... It was a blow. The harshest form of rejection I could ever have fathomed, but I needed it. I didn't know it, but I did. It opened me up, and allowed me to be who I am today. Allowed me to fall for you. I mean could you have imagined that would have been possible? That this would be the outcome? Us?
JULIAN. No, I swear to God.
SHELLY. Me neither. Look, there is absolutely zero chance I have a single emotion attached to that situation. Nothing bad can come of this. Seriously, I just want to say hello to him. *(Shelly moves for the door.)*
JULIAN. It's just ...
SHELLY. Unethical under the circumstances, I know. I think he

of all people will understand. *(She opens the door. Terry sees her and freezes. They stare at each other for what seems like an eternity.)* Hi Terry.

TERRY. Hi Shelly. *(Terry walks onto the stage very slowly.)*

SHELLY. It's really good to see you.

TERRY. It's good to see ... *(Terry turns to Julian.)* What is this?

JULIAN. This is completely inappropriate, you're right. This is not something we should do here.

TERRY. Do what? What are we doing here?

SHELLY. Nothing. I'm sorry. This is my fault. I just wanted to say hello to you. I've done that, and now I'm going to leave. It was nice seeing you, Terry.

TERRY. Wait a minute. What are you doing here? What is she doing here?

SHELLY. Excuse me?

TERRY. I thought you said she stopped coming to see you a long time ago.

JULIAN. She did.

TERRY. Then what is she doing here?

SHELLY. I was bringing him his lunch, thank you. And when did my personal life become any of his business, Julian?

JULIAN. It didn't. It's not.

TERRY. Bringing him his lunch?

SHELLY. Stay out of this, please. Julian, I'm asking you a question.

JULIAN. I just answered it.

TERRY. Excuse me, I believe this is my time.

SHELLY. You're early; if you'd like to continue waiting in the waiting room, please be my guest. I just thought I would be polite and say hello.

TERRY. Polite? Come on with the polite. Now you have tact, and manners.

SHELLY. Me? Wow, do you have nerve.

TERRY. I have nerve?

SHELLY. That's what I said. You have nerve.

TERRY. I know that. I was repeating it because I didn't believe you actually said it, not because I literally didn't hear you. I heard what you said.

SHELLY. Great. You're so witty and clever.

JULIAN. Okay. This is over. Shelly, we can discuss anything you feel that we need to discuss later. Right now, truth be told, give or take a minute or so, Terry is right, this is his time.

SHELLY. Fine. You know what … Forget it. Take your time. Take it slowly and well, because as far as I'm concerned, you need every last minute you can get.

JULIAN. Shelly, that's enough.

TERRY. What the hell is that supposed to mean?

SHELLY. Are you being clever again, or do you really need me to decipher what was just said? You need help. Get it now?

TERRY. Would you get out of here? Take his lunch, crazy lady, whatever that means, and get the hell out.

SHELLY. Are you going to let him speak to me this way?

JULIAN. This is unusual.

TERRY. Let him speak to you this way? He's a doctor, not a teacher. This isn't a classroom. We're in the real world here where people speak to each other. One on one. There's no middle man in conversations, nor in relationships. I speak what I feel here, and I speak it to you, the person I am speaking to. You see how that works?

SHELLY. *(Shelly grabs the first thing she sees and tosses it at Terry's head. He ducks.)* Asshole!

TERRY. We also don't throw things here in this land I speak of.

SHELLY. Where the hell do you get off?

TERRY. You just called me an asshole and threw something at my head. Where do I get off? Here seems like it might be a good place. Good thing you're back here. Doc, she needs you. Now it's all making sense. *(Shelly grabs something else off of the desk.)*

SHELLY. Son of a bitch.

TERRY. Hey, hey. *(Terry backs up. Julian steps in between them.)*

JULIAN. Okay. Terry, please sit down.

TERRY. Sit down? She's just grabbed another object, sir. Sitting down seems to be a bad idea at this point. Defensively, I mean. *(Julian turns to Shelly, who is fuming.)*

JULIAN. Babe, I'm begging you to walk out the door. This is something else here, and I'm begging you to let me handle this.

TERRY. I'm sorry, did you just say babe?

JULIAN. No.

SHELLY. Julian.

JULIAN. Did I?

SHELLY. Yeah, he called me babe. As in baby. As in oh baby, right there don't stop.

JULIAN. Oh my God.

SHELLY. Oh, man up, Julian. Jesus Christ.

TERRY. So that's lunch huh?

SHELLY. Lunch, breakfast and dinner too, pal. *(Julian sits down.)*

JULIAN. Oh my God. *(Terry looks around the room, and puts it together.)*

TERRY. Okay. First of all, you're fired ... Yeah, that's for sure. *(Terry turns to Shelly.)* You. Just tell me you're crazy. That I can live with.

SHELLY. I've never been so healthy in all my life. A shame for you really, but I guess we'll never know.

TERRY. Never know what? What are you saying? Is that code?

SHELLY. Yeah, it's code.

TERRY. Well?

SHELLY. You know if you were scared, or if you just plain didn't like me, I would have listened. Either way it could have been fine. Different at least. Not like this anyway.

TERRY. Excuse me, but what the fuck are you talking about?

JULIAN. I should probably say something here.

TERRY. You might like to get kicked in the teeth if you say something here, so I'd like to sit right there if I was you. Babe? How can she be babe?

JULIAN. I'm sorry.

SHELLY. Don't you apologize to him.

TERRY. Someone needs to, I'd rather it be you, truth be told.

SHELLY. Me? Me? Me?

TERRY. What, are you tuning a piano? Yes, you!

JULIAN. Things happen, Terry.

TERRY. You're not here, okay.

SHELLY. Yes, he is. We're all here. This is an office, and you are a patient. Take this time. Seriously.

TERRY. Wait a minute. Hold on. You know what? I'm all backwards here.

SHELLY. Now you seem to be sobering.

TERRY. Listen here, lunch. He's an asshole, obviously. I should have listened when he said you were crazy, but that was before he was an asshole. So, good luck. You guys will get on just fine, I'm sure.

SHELLY. You told him I was crazy?

JULIAN. It was a long time ago.

TERRY. Hey! Crazy's crazy. Today, tomorrow. It's not the flu. Crazy's crazy.

JULIAN. I never said she was crazy. Exactly.

SHELLY. What exactly did you say?

TERRY. That you were crazy, and that I was better off. Exactly.

JULIAN. In so many words.

TERRY. That many. She's crazy. One two.

SHELLY. Why did you tell him that?

JULIAN. I did not say that.

TERRY. No, first he told me that you were completely sane but that was before I knew you, and actually thought you were crazy. Then when I thought you were sane and had formed an emotional attachment to you, he gave me a twenty-minute metaphor about a rodeo, implying your insanity, then at the end of it said I was better off.

JULIAN. I never said that. I said it could be good luck and it could be …

TERRY. Bad luck. Yeah, I remember. Good luck for you, apparently. *(Shelly takes a second to let it seep in.)*

SHELLY. Is that why you told him you didn't want to see me again?

TERRY. You know, since meeting you a year ago, I have said so many things about you. Truthfully, a lot of them not very nice. Hours and hours in this very room. All sorts of things. Never wanting to see you again was not one of them, though. *(Shelly turns to Julian.)*

SHELLY. Did you do this?

JULIAN. This is not … For this time … Here … This is not what it seems.

SHELLY. Then, tell me what it is.

TERRY. I think it might be worse than what it seems.

JULIAN. That might be true.

SHELLY. What the hell is going on?

TERRY. Did you tell him that you didn't want to see or speak to me ever again?

SHELLY. Yes.

TERRY. Great. Awesome. I'm leaving.

SHELLY. But only after he told me what you said.

TERRY. Which part, because I'm confused. Like I said, I said a lot of things. How calm I felt around you. How at ease. How it seemed like I was with a friend that I wanted sexually. The part about you being perfect in every way, or was it something else that set you off.

SHELLY. I'm confused.

JULIAN. I'm going to explain.

41

TERRY. I'm going to kill.

SHELLY. Why didn't you ever call?

TERRY. Why didn't you?

SHELLY. I don't know.

TERRY. Neither do I.

JULIAN. Can we all sit? *(Shelly and Terry slowly sit down.)* I'm actually going to stand ... Terry?

TERRY. What?

JULIAN. How long have you been single now?

TERRY. About nine months.

JULIAN. How do you feel?

TERRY. What is this, group?

JULIAN. I'm cushioning my own fall here, please allow this.

TERRY. I feel fine.

JULIAN. First time?

TERRY. No, I've felt fine before.

JULIAN. Being single.

TERRY. Yes. *(Terry takes a few seconds.)*

JULIAN. Babe? *(Julian turns to Shelly.)*

TERRY. Boy, does that make me sick.

SHELLY. Shelly for now, dear.

JULIAN. Fine. We've been together for almost nine months.

TERRY. Oh my God!

SHELLY. Yes.

JULIAN. Did you ever think that was possible? With me, or anyone for that matter?

SHELLY. *(Shelly takes a few seconds.)* No.

JULIAN. Relationships, in any form, are a constant struggle. They are never flawless, and it is a neverending work. Perfection does not exist. You never know how things will end up, begin, or continue. I only say this to exonerate myself partially. I've done a very bad thing. But I'm only a human being. I have feelings and I don't live in this office. I lied and I cheated the both of you. Shelly, I love you. Terry, I'm sorry. *(Lights out.)*

End of Act Three

CLEAN UP

The waiting room of a therapist's office — some time later.

Lights up. Terry, calmly sits alone in the waiting room. After a few beats, Shelly walks in.

TERRY. Hey.
SHELLY. Sorry I'm late.
TERRY. No, you're right on time. *(They sit in silence for a few beats. Terry catches her eye and cracks a smile. Shelly smiles back. Their smiles turn into subtle laughing. A shared knowledge of what has happened and excitement for what is to come. He leans over and kisses her on the lips. She holds his hand. Both still smiling. The door to the office opens and Julian pops his head out.)*
JULIAN. You guys ready to get started? *(Shelly and Terry take a beat, and then stand together. Julian holds the door, and as Shelly moves into the office, he tilts his head down, subtly checking her out. Not subtle enough. Terry catches this, walks past Julian, and lightly slaps him on the back of his head as he enters the office.)*
TERRY. Hey. *(Julian half smiles, then almost to himself ...)*
JULIAN. Sorry. *(Then enters the office following the couple. Lights out.)*

End of Play

PROPERTY LIST

2 coffees
Book
Paper bag with lunch

NEW PLAYS

★ **AT HOME AT THE ZOO by Edward Albee.** Edward Albee delves deeper into his play THE ZOO STORY by adding a first act, HOMELIFE, which precedes Peter's fateful meeting with Jerry on a park bench in Central Park. "An essential and heartening experience." —*NY Times.* "Darkly comic and thrilling." —*Time Out.* "Genuinely fascinating." —*Journal News.* [2M, 1W] ISBN: 978-0-8222-2317-7

★ **PASSING STRANGE book and lyrics by Stew, music by Stew and Heidi Rodewald, created in collaboration with Annie Dorsen.** A daring musical about a young bohemian that takes you from black middle-class America to Amsterdam, Berlin and beyond on a journey towards personal and artistic authenticity. "Fresh, exuberant, bracingly inventive, bitingly funny, and full of heart." —*NY Times.* "The freshest musical in town!" —*Wall Street Journal.* "Excellent songs and a vulnerable heart." —*Variety.* [4M, 3W] ISBN: 978-0-8222-2400-6

★ **REASONS TO BE PRETTY by Neil LaBute.** Greg really, truly adores his girlfriend, Steph. Unfortunately, he also thinks she has a few physical imperfections, and when he mentions them, all hell breaks loose. "Tight, tense and emotionally true." —*Time Magazine.* "Lively and compulsively watchable." —*The Record.* [2M, 2W] ISBN: 978-0-8222-2394-8

★ **OPUS by Michael Hollinger.** With only a few days to rehearse a grueling Beethoven masterpiece, a world-class string quartet struggles to prepare their highest-profile performance ever—a televised ceremony at the White House. "Intimate, intense and profoundly moving." —*Time Out.* "Worthy of scores of bravissimos." —*BroadwayWorld.com.* [4M, 1W] ISBN: 978-0-8222-2363-4

★ **BECKY SHAW by Gina Gionfriddo.** When an evening calculated to bring happiness takes a dark turn, crisis and comedy ensue in this wickedly funny play that asks what we owe the people we love and the strangers who land on our doorstep. "As engrossing as it is ferociously funny." —*NY Times.* "Gionfriddo is some kind of genius." —*Variety.* [2M, 3W] ISBN: 978-0-8222-2402-0

★ **KICKING A DEAD HORSE by Sam Shepard.** Hobart Struther's horse has just dropped dead. In an eighty-minute monologue, he discusses what path brought him here in the first place, the fate of his marriage, his career, politics and eventually the nature of the universe. "Deeply instinctual and intuitive." —*NY Times.* "The brilliance is in the infinite reverberations Shepard extracts from his simple metaphor." —*TheaterMania.* [1M, 1W] ISBN: 978-0-8222-2336-8

DRAMATISTS PLAY SERVICE, INC.
440 Park Avenue South, New York, NY 10016 212-683-8960 Fax 212-213-1539
postmaster@dramatists.com www.dramatists.com

NEW PLAYS

★ **AUGUST: OSAGE COUNTY by Tracy Letts.** WINNER OF THE 2008 PULITZER PRIZE AND TONY AWARD. When the large Weston family reunites after Dad disappears, their Oklahoma homestead explodes in a maelstrom of repressed truths and unsettling secrets. "Fiercely funny and bitingly sad." *–NY Times.* "Ferociously entertaining." *–Variety.* "A hugely ambitious, highly combustible saga." *–NY Daily News.* [6M, 7W] ISBN: 978-0-8222-2300-9

★ **RUINED by Lynn Nottage.** WINNER OF THE 2009 PULITZER PRIZE. Set in a small mining town in Democratic Republic of Congo, RUINED is a haunting, probing work about the resilience of the human spirit during times of war. "A full-immersion drama of shocking complexity and moral ambiguity." *–Variety.* "Sincere, passionate, courageous." *–Chicago Tribune.* [8M, 4W] ISBN: 978-0-8222-2390-0

★ **GOD OF CARNAGE by Yasmina Reza, translated by Christopher Hampton.** WINNER OF THE 2009 TONY AWARD. A playground altercation between boys brings together their Brooklyn parents, leaving the couples in tatters as the rum flows and tensions explode. "Satisfyingly primitive entertainment." *–NY Times.* "Elegant, acerbic, entertainingly fueled on pure bile." *–Variety.* [2M, 2W] ISBN: 978-0-8222-2399-3

★ **THE SEAFARER by Conor McPherson.** Sharky has returned to Dublin to look after his irascible, aging brother. Old drinking buddies Ivan and Nicky are holed up at the house too, hoping to play some cards. But with the arrival of a stranger from the distant past, the stakes are raised ever higher. "Dark and enthralling Christmas fable." *–NY Times.* "A timeless classic." *–Hollywood Reporter.* [5M] ISBN: 978-0-8222-2284-2

★ **THE NEW CENTURY by Paul Rudnick.** When the playwright is Paul Rudnick, expectations are geared for a play both hilarious and smart, and this provocative and outrageous comedy is no exception. "The one-liners fly like rockets." *–NY Times.* "The funniest playwright around." *–Journal News.* [2M, 3W] ISBN: 978-0-8222-2315-3

★ **SHIPWRECKED! AN ENTERTAINMENT—THE AMAZING ADVENTURES OF LOUIS DE ROUGEMONT (AS TOLD BY HIMSELF) by Donald Margulies.** The amazing story of bravery, survival and celebrity that left nineteenth-century England spellbound. Dare to be whisked away. "A deft, literate narrative." *–LA Times.* "Springs to life like a theatrical pop-up book." *–NY Times.* [2M, 1W] ISBN: 978-0-8222-2341-2

DRAMATISTS PLAY SERVICE, INC.
440 Park Avenue South, New York, NY 10016 212-683-8960 Fax 212-213-1539
postmaster@dramatists.com www.dramatists.com